CAN
DIABETES

Dr. Kimberly Carlos

Copyright © 2023 by Dr. Kimberly Carlos

TABLE OF CONTENT

INTRODUCTION

In a quaint village nestled between rolling hills, lived a woman named Evelyn. She was known for her warm smile, nurturing nature, and a secret skill that made her truly remarkable – canning.

Evelyn had been diagnosed with diabetes at a young age, and she had learned to manage her condition with care and creativity. She embraced canning as a way to maintain a healthy diet while still indulging in the flavors she loved. Her garden overflowed with vibrant fruits and vegetables, which she skillfully preserved in glass jars.

Every summer, the village eagerly awaited Evelyn's canned creations. She would spend hours in her kitchen, carefully peeling, slicing, and seasoning the produce.

She transformed ripe peaches into delectable sugar-free preserves, and turned plump tomatoes into rich, tangy salsa without added sugars. Her pickled cucumbers were a hit at every local gathering.

As word spread about Evelyn's diabetes-friendly canning, people from neighboring villages sought her advice.

She began hosting workshops, teaching others how to create delicious and nutritious canned goods. Her kitchen became a hub of learning and community, a place where people with diabetes and their loved ones could gather to share stories, exchange tips, and learn about managing the condition through food.

Evelyn's journey wasn't without challenges. She faced skeptics who doubted her ability to create flavorful treats without compromising health. But she persevered, experimenting tirelessly to find the perfect combinations of spices, herbs, and natural sweeteners. Her dedication paid off, and her creations were loved not only by those managing diabetes but by everyone who tasted them.

Through her passion for canning, Evelyn transformed her personal struggle into a source of empowerment and connection for her community. She showed that with determination, creativity, and a bit of culinary magic, managing diabetes could be a delicious journey.

And in doing so, she turned her kitchen into a place of inspiration, where jars of hope and flavors of resilience were preserved for generations to come.

CHAPTER ONE

Types, Causes and Symptoms of Diabetes

Types of Diabetes

1. Type 1 Diabetes (T1D)

- **Cause:** Type 1 diabetes is an autoimmune condition where the immune system mistakenly attacks and destroys the insulin-producing cells in the pancreas. The exact cause is still unknown, but genetics and environmental factors are thought to play a role.

- **Symptoms:** Rapid onset of symptoms, often in children or young adults. Excessive thirst, frequent urination, unexplained weight loss, extreme hunger, fatigue, and blurred vision are common signs.

2. Type 2 Diabetes (T2D)

- **Cause:** Type 2 diabetes typically develops when the body becomes resistant to insulin, and the pancreas struggles to produce enough insulin to compensate. Lifestyle factors such as poor diet, lack of physical activity, obesity, and genetics contribute to its development.

- **Symptoms:** Gradual onset of symptoms. Increased thirst, frequent urination, fatigue, slow-healing wounds, frequent infections, and blurred vision are often observed.

3. Gestational Diabetes

- **Cause:** Gestational diabetes occurs during pregnancy when hormonal changes can lead to insulin resistance. The exact cause is not fully understood, but hormones from the placenta are thought to play a role.
- **Symptoms:** Often asymptomatic, but increased thirst, frequent urination, and fatigue might be observed. It usually resolves after childbirth, but women who experience it have a higher risk of developing type 2 diabetes later in life.

4. Monogenic Diabetes

- **Cause:** Caused by mutations in a single gene, monogenic diabetes is relatively rare and often runs in families. It can present similarly to both type 1 and type 2 diabetes.
- **Symptoms:** Can vary widely, but they generally include elevated blood sugar levels and typical diabetes symptoms.

5. Secondary Diabetes

- **Cause:** Secondary diabetes is the result of an underlying medical condition or medication that impairs insulin function. Conditions like pancreatic diseases or hormonal disorders can lead to secondary diabetes.
- **Symptoms:** Symptoms align with the underlying condition causing diabetes. Blood sugar levels are typically elevated.

Common Symptoms of Diabetes

- Excessive thirst and hunger
- Frequent urination
- Fatigue
- Unexplained weight loss (more prominent in type 1)
- Blurred vision
- Slow-healing wounds or infections
- Tingling or numbness in extremities (diabetic neuropathy)

Diabetes is a complex and diverse condition, with different types stemming from various causes. It's crucial to understand the type of diabetes one has to effectively manage it through lifestyle changes, medications, and, in some cases, insulin therapy. Regular medical check-ups, monitoring blood sugar levels, and adopting a healthy lifestyle are essential components of diabetes management regardless of its type.

Diabetes Diet with Benefits

Living with diabetes demands a thoughtful and intentional approach to diet and lifestyle. One strategy that has gained popularity is canning, a culinary art that allows individuals to preserve and enjoy the bounty of fruits and vegetables while adhering to diabetes management guidelines. Canning for diabetes isn't just about preserving food; it's a way to craft nourishing, flavorful creations that support blood sugar control, provide essential nutrients, and offer a myriad of benefits for overall health.

The Basics of Canning

Canning involves preserving foods by sealing them in airtight containers, usually glass jars, to prevent spoilage and maintain freshness. The two main methods of canning are water bath canning and pressure canning. Water bath canning is suitable for high-acid foods like fruits, jams, and pickles, while pressure canning is necessary for low-acid foods like vegetables, meats, and poultry.

Benefits of Canning for Diabetes

1. Portion Control: Canning allows you to portion out your foods into controlled servings. This assists in managing carbohydrate intake, a crucial aspect of diabetes management, and prevents overeating.

2. Nutrient Preservation: Canned foods retain a significant amount of their original nutrients, vitamins, and minerals. This is particularly important for individuals with diabetes, as nutrient balance can contribute to stable blood sugar levels.

3. Reduced Added Sugars: Canning empowers you to create delicious jams, jellies, and preserves without excessive added sugars. Natural sweeteners like stevia, erythritol, or even the fruit's own sugars can be used to enhance flavors without causing spikes in blood sugar.

4. Controlled Ingredients: When canning at home, you have complete control over the ingredients you use. This means you can avoid artificial additives, excess salt, and other components that might not align with a diabetes-friendly diet.

5. Year-Round Accessibility: Canning allows you to enjoy seasonal produce throughout the year. You can capture the flavors of ripe summer fruits or hearty autumn vegetables and savor them during any season.

6. Customization: You can adjust recipes to suit your specific dietary needs and taste preferences. Whether you're following a low-carb, low-sodium, or high-fiber diet, canning can be tailored to your requirements.

Tips for Canning with Diabetes in Mind:

1. Choose High-Quality Ingredients: Opt for fresh, ripe produce to ensure the best flavor and nutrient content in your canned goods.

2. Monitor Carbohydrates: Keep track of the carbohydrate content of the ingredients you're using. This will help you manage portion sizes and calculate insulin requirements if necessary.

3. Use Natural Sweeteners: Experiment with natural sweeteners like stevia, monk fruit, or erythritol to reduce added sugars while maintaining sweetness.

4. Incorporate Fiber: Fiber helps slow down the absorption of sugars, promoting stable blood sugar levels. Add high-fiber ingredients like chia seeds, flaxseeds, or fruits rich in fiber.

5. Control Sodium: If a recipe calls for salt, consider using a reduced-sodium option or omitting it altogether.

6. Practice Safe Canning: Follow proper canning techniques to ensure food safety. Sterilize jars, use tested recipes, and adhere to processing times and methods.

7. Diversify Your Creations: Canning isn't limited to jams; explore salsas, chutneys, relishes, and more. These can add exciting flavors to your meals without compromising your diabetes management.

Embracing canning for diabetes isn't just a culinary choice; it's a lifestyle decision that can lead to healthier eating habits, improved blood sugar control, and a broader appreciation for the goodness of whole foods.

By incorporating fresh ingredients, mindful preparation, and diabetes-conscious choices, you can create a pantry filled with flavorful delights that contribute to your overall well-being.

CHAPTER TWO

14-Day Canning for Diabetes Meal Plan

Day 1

- Breakfast: Greek yogurt with canned sugar-free mixed berry compote and a sprinkle of chopped nuts.
- Lunch: Canned vegetable soup with whole grain crackers and a side salad.
- Dinner: Canned salsa-marinated grilled chicken with quinoa and steamed vegetables.

Day 2

- Breakfast: Canned fruit salad with cottage cheese and a drizzle of honey.
- Lunch: Canned tuna salad with mixed greens, cherry tomatoes, and a vinaigrette dressing.
- Dinner: Canned tomato-based vegetable curry with brown rice.

Day 3

- Breakfast: Overnight oats made with canned peaches, almond milk, and chia seeds.
- Lunch: Canned black bean and corn salad with diced avocado and lime dressing.
- Dinner: Canned salmon cakes with mashed cauliflower and steamed broccoli.

Day 4

- Breakfast: Whole grain toast topped with canned sugar-free apple butter and almond butter.
- Lunch: Canned roasted red pepper and tomato soup with a side of whole grain bread.
- Dinner: Canned ratatouille with grilled lean protein (chicken or tofu).

Day 5

- Breakfast: Canned mixed berry smoothie with spinach, Greek yogurt, and a splash of almond milk.
- Lunch: Canned white bean and roasted vegetable wrap with a side of carrot sticks.
- Dinner: Canned vegetable stir-fry with lean protein and brown rice.

Day 6

- Breakfast: Scrambled eggs with diced canned tomatoes, bell peppers, and onions.
- Lunch: Canned chicken and vegetable salad with a balsamic vinaigrette.
- Dinner: Canned chili with lean ground turkey, served with a side of mixed greens.

Day 7

- Breakfast: Canned pumpkin spice oatmeal topped with chopped nuts and a sprinkle of cinnamon.
- Lunch: Canned chickpea and vegetable stew with a whole grain roll.
- Dinner: Canned vegetable and lentil curry with quinoa.

Day 8

- Breakfast: Whole grain waffles topped with canned mixed berry compote and a dollop of Greek yogurt.
- Lunch: Canned vegetable and bean burrito bowl with avocado and salsa.
- Dinner: Canned teriyaki-glazed salmon with brown rice and steamed asparagus.

Day 9

- Breakfast: Canned fruit parfait with layers of Greek yogurt, granola, and canned fruit.
- Lunch: Canned minestrone soup with whole grain bread and a side salad.
- Dinner: Canned eggplant and tomato pasta sauce over whole wheat pasta.

Day 10

- Breakfast: Omelette with canned spinach and feta cheese, served with whole grain toast.
- Lunch: Canned lentil and vegetable salad with a lemon herb dressing.
- Dinner: Canned vegetable and shrimp stir-fry with cauliflower rice.

Day 11

- Breakfast: Greek yogurt with canned sugar-free mixed berry compote and a sprinkle of chopped nuts.
- Lunch: Canned vegetable soup with whole grain crackers and a side salad.
- Dinner: Canned salsa-marinated grilled chicken with quinoa and steamed vegetables.

Day 12

- Breakfast: Canned fruit salad with cottage cheese and a drizzle of honey.
- Lunch: Canned tuna salad with mixed greens, cherry tomatoes, and a vinaigrette dressing.
- Dinner: Canned tomato-based vegetable curry with brown rice.

Day 13

- Breakfast: Overnight oats made with canned peaches, almond milk, and chia seeds.
- Lunch: Canned black bean and corn salad with diced avocado and lime dressing.
- Dinner: Canned salmon cakes with mashed cauliflower and steamed broccoli.

Day 14

- Breakfast: Whole grain toast topped with canned sugar-free apple butter and almond butter.
- Lunch: Canned roasted red pepper and tomato soup with a side of whole grain bread.
- Dinner: Canned ratatouille with grilled lean protein (chicken or tofu).

CHAPTER THREE

Canning For Diabetes Breakfast Recipes

1. Canned Mixed Berry Parfait

Ingredients:

- 1/2 cup canned mixed berries (in water or own juices)
- 1/2 cup Greek yogurt (low-fat or non-fat)
- 2 tablespoons granola (low-sugar)
- 1 teaspoon honey (optional)

Instructions:

1. In a glass or jar, layer half of the Greek yogurt at the bottom.

2. Spoon half of the canned mixed berries over the yogurt layer.

3. Sprinkle half of the granola on top of the berries.

4. Repeat the layers with the remaining yogurt, berries, and granola.

5. Drizzle with honey if desired.

6. Enjoy immediately or refrigerate for later.

Cooking Time: 10 minutes

2. Canned Fruit Smoothie Bowl

Ingredients:

- 1/2 cup canned fruit (such as peaches, pineapples, or mangoes)
- 1/2 banana, frozen
- 1/2 cup almond milk (unsweetened)
- 1 tablespoon chia seeds
- Toppings: sliced almonds, shredded coconut, berries

Instructions:

1. Blend canned fruit, frozen banana, almond milk, and chia seeds until smooth.

2. Pour the smoothie into a bowl.

3. Top with sliced almonds, shredded coconut, and fresh berries.

4. Enjoy with a spoon.

Cooking Time: 5 minutes

3. Canned Pumpkin Spice Oatmeal

Ingredients:

- 1/2 cup rolled oats
- 1 cup water or milk (dairy or non-dairy)
- 1/4 cup canned pumpkin puree
- 1/2 teaspoon pumpkin spice
- 1 teaspoon maple syrup or honey (optional)

Instructions:

1. In a saucepan, bring water or milk to a boil.

2. Stir in the rolled oats and reduce the heat to simmer.

3. Add the canned pumpkin puree and pumpkin spice, stirring well.

4. Cook until the oats are tender and the mixture thickens.

5. Sweeten with maple syrup or honey if desired.

6. Serve warm.

Cooking Time: 10 minutes

4. Canned Fruit and Yogurt Parfait

Ingredients:

- 1/2 cup canned fruit (such as pears, cherries, or mandarin oranges)
- 1/2 cup plain Greek yogurt (low-fat or non-fat)
- 2 tablespoons chopped nuts (almonds, walnuts, or pistachios)
- 1 teaspoon flaxseeds (ground)

Instructions:

1. In a glass or jar, layer half of the Greek yogurt at the bottom.

2. Add half of the canned fruit on top of the yogurt.

3. Sprinkle with half of the chopped nuts and flaxseeds.

4. Repeat the layers with the remaining yogurt, fruit, nuts, and flaxseeds.

5. Serve immediately.

Cooking Time: 5 minutes

5. Canned Veggie and Cheese Omelette

Ingredients:

- 2 eggs
- 2 tablespoons canned diced tomatoes (drained)
- 2 tablespoons canned spinach (drained)
- 2 tablespoons shredded low-fat cheese (cheddar or mozzarella)
- Salt and pepper to taste
- Cooking spray or a touch of oil

Instructions:

1. In a bowl, beat the eggs with salt and pepper.

2. Heat a non-stick skillet over medium heat and lightly grease with cooking spray or oil.

3. Pour the beaten eggs into the skillet and let them cook until slightly set.

4. Sprinkle the canned diced tomatoes, canned spinach, and shredded cheese over one half of the omelette.

5. Fold the other half of the omelette over the fillings.

6. Cook until the cheese is melted and the omelette is cooked through.

7. Slide the omelette onto a plate and serve.

Cooking Time: 15 minutes

Canning for Diabetes Lunch Recipes

1. Canned Vegetable and Bean Salad

Ingredients:

- 1 cup canned mixed vegetables (drained)
- 1/2 cup canned kidney beans (rinsed and drained)
- 1/4 cup diced red onion
- 2 tablespoons balsamic vinegar
- 1 tablespoon olive oil
- Salt and pepper to taste
- Fresh herbs (such as parsley or basil) for garnish

Instructions:

1. In a bowl, combine the canned mixed vegetables and kidney beans.

2. Add the diced red onion, balsamic vinegar, and olive oil.

3. Season with salt and pepper and toss to combine.

4. Let the flavors meld for a few minutes before serving.

5. Garnish with fresh herbs.

Cooking Time: 10 minutes

2. Canned Tuna Salad Lettuce Wraps

Ingredients:

- 1 can tuna (packed in water, drained)
- 2 tablespoons canned diced celery
- 2 tablespoons canned diced pickles
- 2 tablespoons plain Greek yogurt (low-fat or non-fat)
- Lettuce leaves for wrapping
- Salt and pepper to taste

Instructions:

1. In a bowl, mix the canned tuna, diced celery, diced pickles, and Greek yogurt.

2. Season with salt and pepper to taste.

3. Spoon the tuna salad into lettuce leaves.

4. Roll the leaves to create wraps.

5. Serve immediately.

Cooking Time: 10 minutes

3. Canned Tomato and Roasted Red Pepper Soup

Ingredients:

- 1 can diced tomatoes (no salt added)
- 1/2 cup canned roasted red peppers (drained)
- 1/2 onion, diced
- 1 clove garlic, minced
- 1 cup low-sodium vegetable broth
- 1/2 teaspoon dried basil
- 1/2 teaspoon dried oregano
- Salt and pepper to taste

Instructions:

1. In a pot, sauté the diced onion and minced garlic until translucent.

2. Add the canned diced tomatoes, canned roasted red peppers, vegetable broth, basil, and oregano.

3. Simmer for about 15 minutes to allow the flavors to meld.

4. Use an immersion blender to blend the soup until smooth.

5. Season with salt and pepper to taste.

6. Heat the soup before serving.

Cooking Time: 20 minutes

4. Canned Chickpea and Vegetable Stir-Fry

Ingredients:

- 1 can chickpeas (rinsed and drained)
- 1 cup canned mixed vegetables (drained)
- 1/2 bell pepper, sliced
- 1/2 onion, sliced
- 2 tablespoons low-sodium soy sauce
- 1 tablespoon sesame oil
- 1/2 teaspoon minced ginger
- 1/2 teaspoon minced garlic
- Sesame seeds for garnish

Instructions:

1. In a pan, heat sesame oil and sauté the sliced onion, bell pepper, minced ginger, and minced garlic.

2. Add the canned chickpeas and canned mixed vegetables.

3. Pour in the low-sodium soy sauce and stir-fry for a few minutes.

4. Garnish with sesame seeds before serving.

Cooking Time: 15 minutes

5. Canned Chicken and Vegetable Wrap

Ingredients:

- 1 can canned chicken (drained)
- 1/4 cup canned diced carrots
- 1/4 cup canned corn (drained)
- 2 tablespoons plain Greek yogurt (low-fat or non-fat)
- Whole grain wrap or tortilla
- Lettuce and tomato slices for filling

Instructions:

1. In a bowl, mix the canned chicken, diced carrots, canned corn, and Greek yogurt.

2. Lay out the whole grain wrap or tortilla.

3. Add lettuce and tomato slices on the wrap.

4. Spoon the chicken and vegetable mixture onto the wrap.

5. Roll the wrap tightly.

6. Cut in half and enjoy.

Cooking Time: 10 minutes

CHAPTER FOUR

Canning for Diabetes Dinner Recipes

1. Canned Vegetable and Lentil Stew

Ingredients:

- 1 cup canned mixed vegetables (drained)
- 1/2 cup canned lentils (rinsed and drained)
- 1/2 cup low-sodium vegetable broth
- 1/4 cup canned diced tomatoes (no salt added)
- 1/2 onion, diced
- 1 carrot, diced
- 1 celery stalk, diced
- 1/2 teaspoon dried thyme
- Salt and pepper to taste

Instructions:

1. In a pot, sauté the diced onion, carrot, and celery until softened.

2. Add the canned mixed vegetables, canned lentils, canned diced tomatoes, and vegetable broth.

3. Season with dried thyme, salt, and pepper.

4. Simmer the stew for about 15-20 minutes to allow the flavors to meld.

5. Adjust the seasoning if needed and serve.

Cooking Time: 25 minutes

2. Canned Teriyaki-Glazed Salmon

Ingredients:

- 2 salmon fillets
- 1/4 cup canned pineapple chunks (in juice)
- 2 tablespoons low-sodium teriyaki sauce
- 1 tablespoon low-sodium soy sauce
- 1 teaspoon minced ginger
- 1 teaspoon minced garlic
- Sesame seeds and sliced green onions for garnish

Instructions:

1. In a bowl, combine the low-sodium teriyaki sauce, low-sodium soy sauce, minced ginger, and minced garlic.

2. Place the salmon fillets in a shallow dish and pour the teriyaki mixture over them. Marinate for about 20 minutes.

3. Preheat the grill or oven to medium-high heat.

4. Grill or bake the salmon fillets until cooked through, basting with the marinade.

5. In a separate bowl, combine the canned pineapple chunks (drained) for a salsa-like topping.

6. Serve the teriyaki-glazed salmon topped with the canned pineapple salsa, sesame seeds, and sliced green onions.

Cooking Time: 20 minutes

3. Canned Ratatouille with Quinoa

Ingredients:

- 1 cup canned diced tomatoes (no salt added)
- 1/2 cup canned eggplant cubes
- 1/2 cup canned zucchini slices
- 1/2 cup canned bell pepper strips
- 1/4 cup canned onion slices
- 2 cloves garlic, minced
- 1 teaspoon dried basil
- 1 teaspoon dried oregano
- Salt and pepper to taste

- Cooked quinoa for serving

Instructions:

1. In a pot, sauté the minced garlic until fragrant.

2. Add the canned diced tomatoes, canned eggplant, canned zucchini, canned bell pepper, and canned onion.

3. Season with dried basil, dried oregano, salt, and pepper.

4. Simmer the mixture for about 15 minutes to allow the flavors to meld.

5. Serve the ratatouille over cooked quinoa.

Cooking Time: 20 minutes

4. Canned Vegetable and Shrimp Stir-Fry

Ingredients:

- 1 cup canned mixed vegetables (drained)
- 1/2 cup canned baby corn (drained)
- 1/2 cup canned bamboo shoots (drained)
- 1/2 cup cooked and peeled shrimp
- 2 tablespoons low-sodium stir-fry sauce
- 1 tablespoon low-sodium soy sauce

- 1 teaspoon sesame oil
- 1/2 teaspoon minced ginger
- 1/2 teaspoon minced garlic

Instructions:

1. Heat sesame oil in a pan or wok over medium-high heat.

2. Add minced ginger and minced garlic, sautéing until fragrant.

3. Stir in the canned mixed vegetables, canned baby corn, and canned bamboo shoots.

4. Add the cooked shrimp and drizzle with low-sodium stir-fry sauce and low-sodium soy sauce.

5. Stir-fry the mixture for a few minutes until heated through.

6. Serve the vegetable and shrimp stir-fry over brown rice or cauliflower rice.

Cooking Time: 15 minutes

5. Canned Tomato-Based Vegetable Curry

Ingredients:

- 1 cup canned diced tomatoes (no salt added)
- 1/2 cup canned chickpeas (rinsed and drained)
- 1/2 cup canned peas (drained)
- 1/2 cup canned potatoes (drained and diced)
- 1/4 cup canned coconut milk (light)
- 1/2 onion, diced
- 1 teaspoon curry powder
- 1/2 teaspoon ground cumin
- 1/2 teaspoon ground coriander
- Salt and pepper to taste
- Fresh cilantro for garnish

Instructions:

1. In a pan, sauté the diced onion until softened.

2. Add the canned diced tomatoes, canned chickpeas, canned peas, and canned potatoes.

3. Season with curry powder, ground cumin, ground coriander, salt, and pepper.

4. Pour in the canned coconut milk and simmer for about 10-15 minutes.

5. Adjust the seasoning if needed and garnish with fresh cilantro before serving.

6. Serve the vegetable curry with brown rice or whole wheat naan.

Cooking Time: 20 minutes

Canning for Diabetes Dessert Recipes

1. Canned Mixed Berry Chia Seed Jam

Ingredients:

- 1 cup canned mixed berries (in water or own juices)
- 2 tablespoons chia seeds
- 1-2 tablespoons honey or a natural sweetener (adjust to taste)

Instructions:

1. In a blender, puree the canned mixed berries until smooth.

2. In a bowl, combine the pureed berries, chia seeds, and honey.

3. Stir well and refrigerate for a few hours, allowing the chia seeds to absorb the liquid and thicken the mixture.

4. Spoon the chia seed jam into sterilized jars and seal.

5. Refrigerate and enjoy as a spread or topping.

Prep Time: 10 minutes (+ chilling time)

2. Canned Fruit Parfait with Yogurt and Nuts

Ingredients:

- 1/2 cup canned fruit (such as peaches, pineapple, or pears)
- 1/2 cup plain Greek yogurt (low-fat or non-fat)
- 2 tablespoons chopped nuts (almonds, walnuts, or pistachios)
- 1 teaspoon honey or a natural sweetener (optional)

Instructions:

1. In a glass or jar, layer half of the Greek yogurt.

2. Add half of the canned fruit on top of the yogurt layer.

3. Sprinkle half of the chopped nuts over the fruit.

4. Repeat the layers with the remaining yogurt, fruit, and nuts.

5. Drizzle with honey if desired.

6. Enjoy as a wholesome dessert.

Prep Time: 5 minutes

3. Canned Pumpkin Spice Parfait with Granola

Ingredients:

- 1/2 cup canned pumpkin puree
- 1/2 cup Greek yogurt (low-fat or non-fat)
- 1/4 teaspoon pumpkin spice
- 2 tablespoons granola (low-sugar)
- 1 teaspoon maple syrup (optional)

Instructions:

1. In a bowl, mix the canned pumpkin puree and Greek yogurt.

2. Stir in the pumpkin spice.

3. In a glass or jar, layer the pumpkin and yogurt mixture with granola.

4. Drizzle with maple syrup if desired.

5. Refrigerate for about 30 minutes to meld the flavors.

6. Enjoy this comforting dessert.

Prep Time: 10 minutes (+ chilling time)

4. Canned Apple Cinnamon Oatmeal Cookies

Ingredients:

- 1/2 cup canned unsweetened applesauce
- 1/2 cup rolled oats
- 1/4 cup whole wheat flour
- 1/2 teaspoon cinnamon
- 1/4 teaspoon baking powder
- 1 tablespoon chopped nuts (optional)

Instructions:

1. Preheat the oven to 350°F (175°C) and line a baking sheet with parchment paper.

2. In a bowl, combine the canned applesauce, rolled oats, whole wheat flour, cinnamon, and baking powder.

3. Drop spoonfuls of the dough onto the baking sheet to form cookies.

4. Sprinkle chopped nuts on top of the cookies.

5. Bake for about 12-15 minutes or until the cookies are lightly golden.

6. Allow the cookies to cool before enjoying.

Cooking Time: 15 minutes

5. Canned Mixed Berry Parfait with Almond Cream

Ingredients:

- 1/2 cup canned mixed berries (in water or own juices)
- 1/4 cup plain Greek yogurt (low-fat or non-fat)
- 2 tablespoons almond butter
- 1 tablespoon crushed almonds
- 1 teaspoon honey or a natural sweetener (optional)

Instructions:

1. In a glass or jar, layer half of the Greek yogurt.

2. Add half of the canned mixed berries on top of the yogurt layer.

3. Dollop a tablespoon of almond butter over the berries.

4. Sprinkle crushed almonds on top of the almond butter.

5. Repeat the layers with the remaining yogurt, berries, almond butter, and almonds.

6. Drizzle with honey if desired.

7. Enjoy this luscious dessert.

Prep Time: 5 minutes

CHAPTER FIVE

Canning for Diabetes Snacks Recipes

1. Canned Veggie and Hummus Dip

Ingredients:

- 1/2 cup canned mixed vegetables (drained)
- 1/4 cup canned chickpeas (rinsed and drained)
- 2 tablespoons tahini
- 1 tablespoon lemon juice
- 1 clove garlic, minced
- Salt and pepper to taste
- Whole grain crackers or vegetable sticks for dipping

Instructions:

1. In a food processor, blend canned mixed vegetables, canned chickpeas, tahini, lemon juice, and minced garlic until smooth.

2. Season with salt and pepper to taste.

3. Serve the veggie and hummus dip with whole grain crackers or vegetable sticks.

Prep Time: 10 minutes

2. Canned Fruit Salsa with Baked Tortilla Chips

Ingredients:

- 1/2 cup canned fruit (such as mangoes, peaches, or pineapple), diced
- 1/4 cup canned black beans (rinsed and drained)
- 2 tablespoons canned diced red onion
- 1 tablespoon lime juice
- 1 tablespoon chopped fresh cilantro
- Salt and pepper to taste
- Baked whole wheat tortilla chips

Instructions:

1. In a bowl, combine canned fruit, canned black beans, canned diced red onion, lime juice, and chopped cilantro.

2. Season with salt and pepper to taste.

3. Serve the fruit salsa with baked whole wheat tortilla chips.

Prep Time: 10 minutes

3. Canned Tuna Cucumber Bites

Ingredients:

- 1 can tuna (packed in water, drained)
- 1/4 cup canned diced celery
- 1/4 cup canned diced pickles
- 2 tablespoons plain Greek yogurt (low-fat or non-fat)
- Cucumber slices

Instructions:

1. In a bowl, mix canned tuna, canned diced celery, canned diced pickles, and Greek yogurt.

2. Spoon the tuna mixture onto cucumber slices.

3. Serve the tuna cucumber bites as a refreshing snack.

Prep Time: 10 minutes

4. Canned Tomato and Avocado Bruschetta

Ingredients:

- 1/2 cup canned diced tomatoes (drained)
- 1/4 cup canned diced red onion
- 1/4 cup canned black beans (rinsed and drained)

- 1 small avocado, diced
- 2 tablespoons chopped fresh basil
- 1 tablespoon balsamic vinegar
- Whole grain baguette slices

Instructions:

1. In a bowl, combine canned diced tomatoes, canned diced red onion, canned black beans, diced avocado, chopped basil, and balsamic vinegar.

2. Mix gently to avoid mashing the avocado.

3. Toast whole grain baguette slices and top with the tomato and avocado mixture.

Prep Time: 15 minutes

5. Canned Nut Butter and Banana Rice Cakes
Ingredients:

- Rice cakes
- 2 tablespoons canned nut butter (almond, peanut, or cashew)
- 1 small banana, sliced

Instructions:

1. Spread a thin layer of canned nut butter on rice cakes.

2. Top with sliced banana.

3. Enjoy the nut butter and banana rice cakes as a quick and satisfying snack.

Prep Time: 5 minutes

Canning for Diabetes Smoothies And Juicing Recipes

1. Canned Mixed Berry Smoothie

Ingredients:

- 1/2 cup canned mixed berries (in water or own juices)
- 1/2 banana, frozen
- 1/2 cup unsweetened almond milk
- 1/2 cup plain Greek yogurt (low-fat or non-fat)
- 1 tablespoon chia seeds
- Ice cubes (optional)

Instructions:

1. Blend canned mixed berries, frozen banana, almond milk, and Greek yogurt until smooth.

2. Add chia seeds and blend briefly to mix.

3. If desired, add ice cubes for extra chilliness.

4. Pour into a glass and enjoy the mixed berry goodness.

Prep Time: 5 minutes

2. Canned Tropical Green Smoothie

Ingredients:

- 1/2 cup canned pineapple chunks (in own juices)
- 1/2 cup canned spinach (drained)
- 1/2 banana, frozen
- 1/2 cup unsweetened coconut milk (or preferred milk)
- 1 tablespoon chia seeds
- Ice cubes (optional)

Instructions:

1. Blend canned pineapple chunks, canned spinach, frozen banana, and coconut milk until smooth.

2. Add chia seeds and blend briefly to combine.

3. If desired, add ice cubes for a cooler texture.

4. Pour into a glass and enjoy the tropical green goodness.

Prep Time: 5 minutes

3. Canned Carrot-Orange Juice

Ingredients:

- 1/2 cup canned carrots (in water or own juices)
- 1 orange, peeled and segmented
- 1/2 lemon, juiced
- 1/2 inch fresh ginger, peeled
- Water or ice cubes as needed

Instructions:

1. Combine canned carrots, orange segments, lemon juice, and fresh ginger in a juicer.

2. Process the ingredients to extract the juice.

3. If the juice is too concentrated, dilute with water or add ice cubes.

4. Pour into a glass and enjoy the zesty carrot-orange blend.

Prep Time: 5 minutes

4. Canned Green Veggie Juice

Ingredients:

- 1/2 cup canned spinach (drained)
- 1/2 cup canned cucumber slices (drained)
- 1/2 cup canned celery (drained)
- 1/2 lemon, juiced
- 1/2 inch fresh ginger, peeled
- Water or ice cubes as needed

Instructions:

1. Combine canned spinach, canned cucumber slices, canned celery, lemon juice, and fresh ginger in a juicer.

2. Process the ingredients to extract the juice.

3. Adjust the consistency by adding water or ice cubes.

4. Pour into a glass and savor the green and refreshing veggie goodness.

Prep Time: 5 minutes

5. Canned Berry Beet Blast Juice

Ingredients:

- 1/2 cup canned mixed berries (in water or own juices)
- 1/4 cup canned beets (drained)
- 1/2 apple, cored and sliced
- 1/2 lemon, juiced
- Water or ice cubes as needed

Instructions:

1. Combine canned mixed berries, canned beets, apple slices, and lemon juice in a juicer.

2. Process the ingredients to extract the juice.

3. Adjust the texture by adding water or ice cubes.

4. Pour into a glass and enjoy the vibrant berry and beet fusion.

Prep Time: 5 minutes

CONCLUSION

In conclusion, canning for diabetes presents a versatile and practical approach to managing blood sugar levels while still enjoying a wide variety of flavorful and nutritious foods. This culinary technique offers a range of benefits that contribute to the well-being of individuals with diabetes.

Through the proper selection and preparation of canned ingredients, individuals can craft meals, snacks, and beverages that align with their dietary requirements and health goals.

Canning empowers individuals to take control of their diabetes management by providing access to an array of fruits, vegetables, legumes, and other ingredients that are preserved at their peak freshness.

Canned goods maintain their nutritional value and flavor, making them a convenient and accessible option for year-round consumption.

This is especially valuable as it ensures that individuals have access to a wide variety of produce, regardless of seasonal availability.

One of the key advantages of canning for diabetes is the preservation of essential nutrients. The canning process locks in vitamins, minerals, and antioxidants, ensuring that these valuable components are retained even during long storage periods.

This is particularly important for individuals with diabetes, as a nutrient-rich diet plays a crucial role in managing blood sugar levels and supporting overall health.

Moreover, canning offers convenience without compromising nutritional quality. With busy lifestyles, meal preparation can be a challenge, but canned ingredients allow for quick and efficient meal assembly.

Whether it's a hearty stew, a refreshing smoothie, or a vibrant salad, canned ingredients streamline the cooking process while delivering valuable nutrients. This convenience not only saves time but also supports adherence to a diabetes-friendly diet.

Canning also provides individuals with diabetes the opportunity to reduce added sugars and sodium in their diet.

By opting for canned goods with no added sugars and selecting low-sodium options, individuals can make informed choices that promote better blood sugar control and lower the risk of related complications.

Canned goods clearly display nutrition labels, enabling individuals to make informed decisions about the nutritional content of their meals.

Furthermore, canning promotes sustainability by reducing food waste. Canned ingredients have a longer shelf life, reducing the likelihood of fresh produce going unused and ultimately ending up in the trash.

This not only benefits individuals by providing a cost-effective option but also contributes to overall food sustainability by minimizing waste.

Incorporating canned ingredients into a diabetes management plan can foster creativity in the kitchen. From breakfast to dinner and snacks in between, there are countless possibilities for crafting delicious and balanced meals that cater to individual taste preferences and nutritional needs.

With the flexibility that canning offers, individuals can experiment with various combinations, flavors, and textures, leading to an enjoyable and sustainable dietary approach.

In conclusion, canning for diabetes is a practical and effective strategy that empowers individuals to create nutritious, diabetes-friendly meals without sacrificing taste or convenience.

By utilizing canned fruits, vegetables, legumes, and more, individuals can enjoy the benefits of nutrient retention, reduced food waste, and the ability to maintain consistent blood sugar levels.

With proper planning and an array of canned ingredients at hand, individuals can embark on a journey of culinary exploration that supports their overall health and well-being, making diabetes management a more enjoyable and sustainable endeavor.

Printed in the USA
CPSIA information can be obtained
at www.ICGtesting.com
CBHW062248110924
14436CB00028B/591